PIANO · VOCAL · GUITAR

BeeGees
Number Ones

D1615232

ISBN 0-634-09691-5

HAL•LEONARD® CORPORATION

7777 W. BLUEMOUND RD. P.O. BOX 13819 MILWAUKEE, WI 53213

0634 096915 3276 3X

MASSACHUSETTS
(The Lights Went Out)

Words and Music by ROBIN GIBB,
MAURICE GIBB and BARRY GIBB

A12 92

Moderately

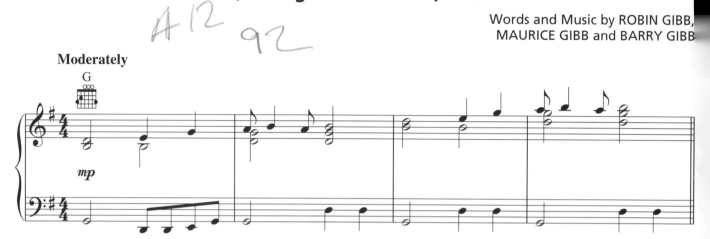

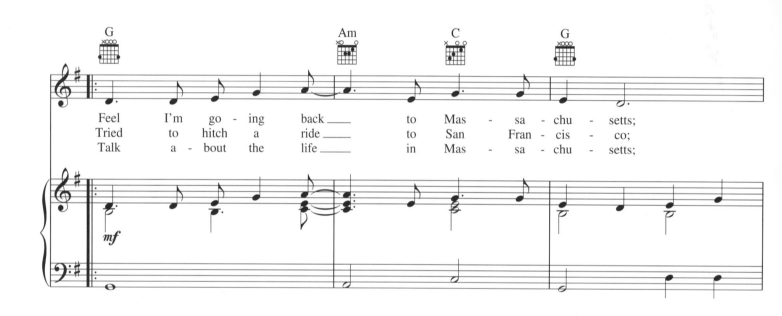

Feel I'm go-ing back ____ to Mas - sa - chu - setts;
Tried to hitch a ride ____ to San Fran - cis - co;
Talk a - bout the life ____ in Mas - sa - chu - setts;

some - thing's tell - ing me ____ I must go
got - ta do the things ____ I wan - na
speak a - bout the peo - ple I have

WORLD

Words and Music by ROBIN GIBB,
MAURICE GIBB and BARRY GIBB

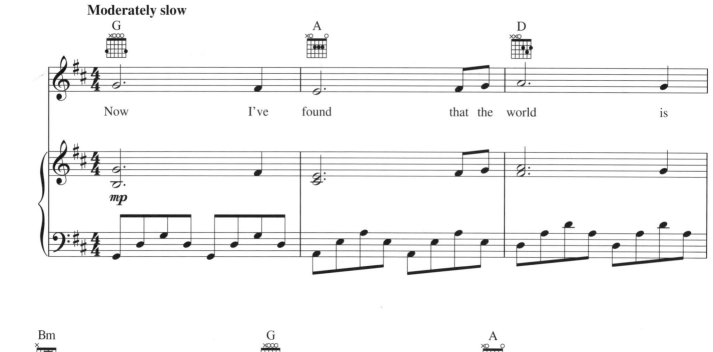

Now I've found that the world is round, and of course it rains ev-'ry day.

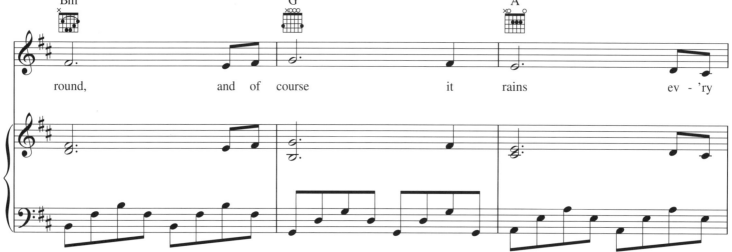

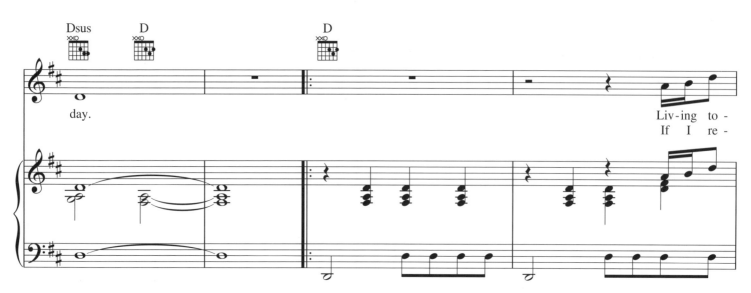

Liv-ing to-
If I re-

DON'T FORGET TO REMEMBER

Words and Music by ROBIN GIBB
and BARRY GIBB

Copyright © 1978 by Gibb Brothers Music, Warner-Tamerlane Publishing Corp. and Crompton Songs LLC
All Rights for Gibb Brothers Music throughout the world Administered by BMG Music Publishing International
All Rights for BMG Music Publishing International in the U.S. Administered by Careers-BMG Music Publishing, Inc.
International Copyright Secured All Rights Reserved

WORDS

Words and Music by ROBIN GIBB,
MAURICE GIBB and BARRY GIBB

Smile an ev - er - last - ing smile; a smile could bring you

near to me. Don't ev - er let me find you

14

I'VE GOTTA GET A MESSAGE TO YOU

Words and Music by ROBIN GIBB,
MAURICE GIBB and BARRY GIBB

I STARTED A JOKE

Words and Music by ROBIN GIBB,
MAURICE GIBB and BARRY GIBB

LONELY DAYS

Words and Music by ROBIN GIBB,
MAURICE GIBB and BARRY GIBB

HOW CAN YOU MEND A BROKEN HEART

Words and Music by ROBIN GIBB
and BARRY GIBB

I can think of young-er days when liv-ing for my life was
I can still feel the breeze that rus-tles through the trees and

ev-'ry-thing a man could want to do.
mist-y mem-o-ries of days gone by.

I could nev-er see to-
We could nev-er see to-

25

JIVE TALKIN'
from SATURDAY NIGHT FEVER

Words and Music by ROBIN GIBB,
MAURICE GIBB and BARRY GIBB

29

YOU SHOULD BE DANCING
from SATURDAY NIGHT FEVER

Words and Music by ROBIN GIBB,
MAURICE GIBB and BARRY GIBB

U33 108

Moderately, with a beat

My ba-by moves at mid-night, _____ goes
juic-y and _____ she's trou-ble, _____ she

right on till the dawn; _____ my wom-an takes me high-er,
gets it to me good; _____ my wom-an give me pow-er,

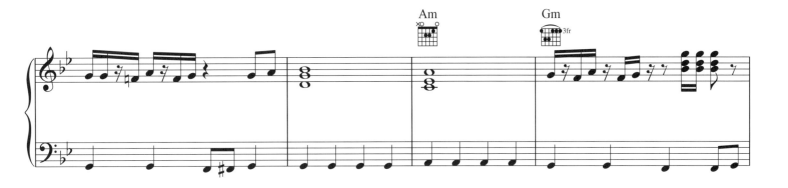

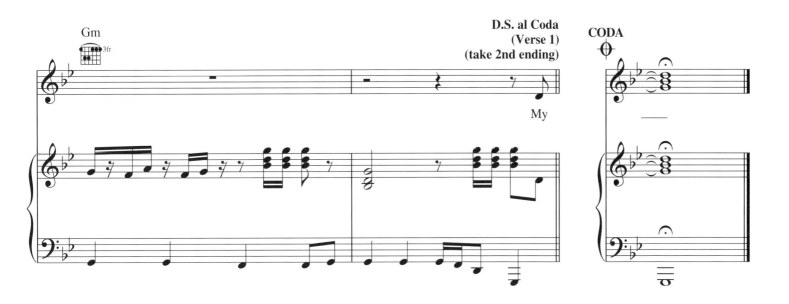

LOVE SO RIGHT

Words and Music by ROBIN GIBB,
MAURICE GIBB and BARRY GIBB

HOW DEEP IS YOUR LOVE
from the Motion Picture SATURDAY NIGHT FEVER

Words and Music by ROBIN GIBB,
MAURICE GIBB and BARRY GIBB

STAYIN' ALIVE
from the Motion Picture SATURDAY NIGHT FEVER

Medium Rock beat

Words and Music by ROBIN GIBB,
MAURICE GIBB and BARRY GIBB

Repeat and Fade

NIGHT FEVER
from SATURDAY NIGHT FEVER

Words and Music by ROBIN GIBB,
MAURICE GIBB and BARRY GIBB

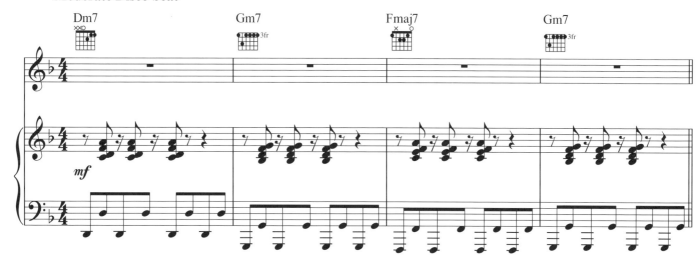

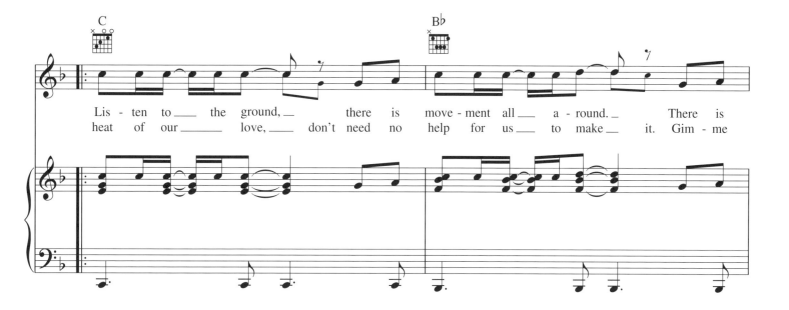

Lis- ten to _ the ground, _ there is move-ment all _ a- round. _ There is
heat of our _ love, _ don't need no help for us _ to make _ it. Gim- me

some- thing go- in' down, _ and I can feel it.   On the
just e- nough to take _ us to the morn- in.'   I got

TOO MUCH HEAVEN

Words and Music by ROBIN GIBB,
MAURICE GIBB and BARRY GIBB

TRAGEDY

Words and Music by ROBIN GIBB,
MAURICE GIBB and BARRY GIBB

Moderate Disco tempo

Here I lie in a lost and lone-ly part of town,
Night and day there's a burn-ing down in-side of me.

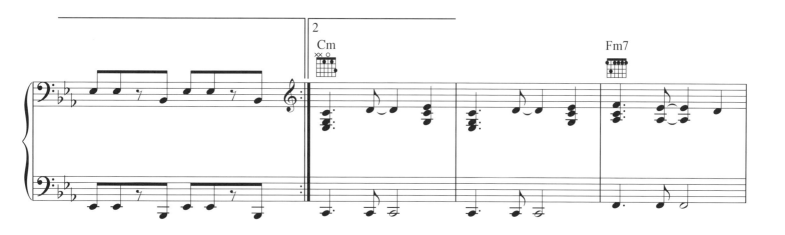

LOVE YOU INSIDE OUT

ABB 84

Words and Music by ROBIN GIBB,
MAURICE GIBB and BARRY GIBB

Moderately

Ba - by, I can't fig - ure it out,___ your kiss - es taste like hon - ey.___

Sweet lies don't gim - me no rise on; oh, what you try - ing to do?___ Liv - in' on___ your

YOU WIN AGAIN

Words and Music by ROBIN GIBB,
MAURICE GIBB and BARRY GIBB

MAN IN THE MIDDLE

Words and Music by ROBIN GIBB,
MAURICE GIBB and BARRY GIBB

That stu-pid man.

No-where to run ___ to; no - where to hide.